EDGE BOOKS

LIBRARY OF WEIRD

THE WORLD'S CRAZIEST RECORDS

by Suzanne Garbe

CAPSTONE PRESS
a capstone imprint

Edge Books are published by Capstone Press,
1710 Roe Crest Drive, North Mankato, Minnesota 56003.
www.capstonepub.com

Library of Congress Cataloging-in-Publication Data
Garbe, Suzanne.
The world's craziest records / by Suzanne Garbe.
pages cm.—(Edge books. Library of weird)
Summary: "Describes some of the craziest, silliest, and most extraordinary records
achieved by people around the world"—Provided by publisher.
Includes bibliographical references and index.
ISBN 978-1-4914-2015-7 (library binding)
ISBN 978-1-4914-2186-4 (ebook PDF)
1. Curiosities and wonders—Juvenile literature. I. Title.
AG243.G297 2015
031.02—dc23   2014014019

Editorial Credits
Aaron Sautter, editor; Kyle Grenz, designer; Charmaine Whitman and Katy
LaVigne, production designers; Pam Mitsakos, media researcher; Kathy McColley,
production specialist

Photo Credits
Alamy: ZUMA Press, Inc., 17; Getty Images: Science Source, 7, Photodisc, 29; Landov:
Reuters/INA FASSBENDER, 27; Newscom: ZUMAPRESS.com/UPPA/Sue Andrews, 11,
ZUMA Press/Ricky Bassman, 19, REUTERS/ALADIN ABDEL NABY, 4–5, ZUMAPRESS.
com/Panoramic/Vukicevic, 12, Zuma Press/UPPA, 13, Photoshot/UPPA/Charlotte
Wiig, 9, Supplied by WENN.com/CB2/ZOB, 18, 24–25, ZUMAPRESS, 23; Shutterstock:
Carlien Beukes, 28, Cidepix, 26, Hurst Photo, 22, Philip Lange, 21, Wayne0216, back
cover; Wikimedia: Krish Dulal, 6, Maria Leijerstam, cover, 15, NASA, 14

Design Elements
Shutterstock: AridOcean, KID_A (throughout)

Direct Quotation
page 12: from "Skydiver Felix Baumgartner Breaks Sound Barrier" by Jonathan Amos for
BBC News, Oct. 14, 2012. http://www.bbc.com/news/science-environment-19943590

Printed in the United States of America in Stevens Point, Wisconsin.
092014   008479WZS15

TABLE OF CONTENTS

CRAZY QUESTS

People have always wanted to do great things. People in ancient times built Stonehenge and the Great Pyramids of Giza. Later on brave adventurers crossed oceans to explore the world. The drive to do great things is still seen today. People build skyscrapers and send robots to Mars. Meanwhile, singers, athletes, and others are honored for their amazing accomplishments.

However, some people don't need to do great things to achieve recognition. Whether they're the world's tallest person or have the world's longest tongue, some people are born to be in the record books. Meanwhile, others often do wild and crazy things to set records. They may ride a lawn mower across the country. They might pull cars using only their hair. Or they try to solve Rubik's Cubes while running marathons. These people usually aren't famous. But their record-setting achievements set them apart as the very best at whatever they do.

Ashrita Furman knows a few things about setting records. Since 1979 he has set 532 world records! Furman is also the current record-holder for holding the most Guinness World Records at one time with 189.

Furman is just one of thousands of people who've pursued the world's craziest records. Learn all about some of the craziest stunts and wildest records ever achieved.

CHAPTER 1

THE HUMAN BODY

Some people are born with extraordinary bodies. They might have extra fingers, stretchy skin, or a super-long tongue. Other people are born with average bodies but turn them into something unusual. Take a look at some of the strangest human body records from around the world.

SHORTEST PERSON

Chandra Bahadur Dangi of Nepal is only 21.5 inches (54.6 centimeters) tall. He was awarded the record at age 72. Three of his siblings are also less than 4 feet (122 cm) tall. However, Dangi also has four other siblings of average height.

HEAVIEST VEHICLE PULLED BY HAIR

In 2012 Asha Rani pulled a bus weighing 26,678 pounds (12,101 kilograms). That's two times the weight of some elephants. But that's not the amazing part. Instead of using her hands, she used her hair! Rani put her hair into two braids, then tied a rope between the braids and the bus. She pulled the bus more than 56 feet (17 meters). Rani earned the nickname "Iron Queen" for her amazing achievement.

TALLEST PERSON

Robert Pershing Wadlow of Alton, Illinois, was the tallest man in history. He measured 8 feet, 11 inches (272 cm) tall. Wadlow was already more than 6 feet (183 cm) tall in third grade. His height was the result of a disorder in his **pituitary gland**. Wadlow was so tall that he needed special braces to help him walk. In 1940 Wadlow died at just 22 years old. He died as a result of an infected blister caused by one of his braces.

pituitary gland—*an organ that influences many body functions, including bone growth*

LONGEST EAR HAIR

Long ear hair is **genetic** and is usually found only in men. It's also more common in elderly people. India's Anthony Victor holds the current world record for longest ear hair at 7.1 inches (18 cm) long.

genetic—*relating to physical traits or conditions passed down from parents to children*

TALLEST MOHAWK

Japanese fashion designer Kazuhiro Watanabe holds the record for the world's tallest mohawk. It takes an entire bottle of gel and three cans of hairspray to hold its height of 44.7 inches (113.5 cm). Watanabe let his hair grow for 15 years to set this record. When it's not in a mohawk, his hair reaches down to his knees.

LONGEST TONGUE

Stephen Taylor of Great Britain has the longest tongue in the world. It measures 3.86 inches (9.8 cm) from the top of his upper lip to the tip! The length of an average tongue is only 0.78 inches (2 cm) long. Taylor does exercises each day to keep his tongue flexible. It's so long that it gives him a **lisp**.

lisp—*a speech problem that causes a person to incorrectly pronounce certain letters, especially "S" and "Z"*

LONGEST FINGERNAILS

Shridhar Chillal of India had the longest fingernails ever measured on a single hand. His nails reached an amazing length of 20 feet, 2.25 inches (6.2 meters)! He began letting his nails grow in 1952 and didn't cut them off until 2000.

MOST WORLD BEARD AND MOUSTACHE CHAMPIONSHIP TITLES

The World Beard and Moustache Championships are held in various locations each year. The contest gives awards for more than 15 beard and moustache styles. Karl-Heinz Hille of Germany has won eight titles at the World Beard and Moustache Championships.

CHAPTER 2
ATHLETIC FEATS

Sports fans can probably name several of their favorite professional athletes. But not all great athletes participate in major sports seen on TV. Some record-holding athletes have much more unusual accomplishments!

A RECORD SWIM

Swimming in the ocean between the United States and Cuba is dangerous. Swimmers here risk attacks by sharks, jellyfish, and other dangerous creatures. In 2013 Diana Nyad became the first person to swim from Cuba to Florida without a shark cage. She first attempted the crossing at age 29 but didn't succeed until her fifth try at age 64. It took Nyad almost 53 hours to complete the journey.

SHOOTING FROM THE FEET

In 2013 Inka Siefker hit a balloon at the center of a target with an arrow. But the amazing part is that she did it with her feet! As Siefker balanced on her hands, she used her feet to shoot the arrow for a record 20 feet (6 m).

DRIBBLING INTO THE RECORD BOOKS

During a 24-hour period in 2001, Suresh Joachim dribbled a basketball for a record 97.4 miles (156.7 km). Joachim holds the second most world records after Ashrita Furman. Joachim's other records include the longest times for watching movies, shaking hands, bowling, drumming, and playing with a band.

A PUZZLING RUNNER

In 2011 Uli Kilian ran the London Marathon to help raise money for cancer research. But he also wanted to set a crazy world record while doing it. As he ran he solved a record 100 Rubik's Cube puzzles in a little less than 5 hours.

HIGHEST BICYCLE TIGHTROPE CROSSING

Acrobat Nik Wallenda rode a bike across a tightrope 238 feet (72.5 m) in the air. That's more than 20 stories high! He held a 30-foot- (9.1-m-) long pole to help him balance. Wallenda also holds the record for being the first person to walk a tightrope across the Grand Canyon in Arizona.

GREATEST FREEFALL DISTANCE

Skydiver Felix Baumgartner made history in 2012. He jumped from a balloon 24 miles (38.6 km) above the Earth. Baumgartner was in **freefall** for nearly 4 ½ minutes before using his parachute. "When I was standing there on top of the world, you become so humble," he told reporters after his achievement. "You don't think about breaking records anymore … the only thing that you want is to come back alive."

DEEPEST FREE IMMERSION DIVE

Free **immersion** divers go deep underwater without oxygen tanks. As they dive they can use only a rope to help pull themselves along. Austrian diver Herbert Nitsch holds the record for the deepest free immersion dive at 394 feet (120 m).

acrobat—*a person who performs gymnastics acts that require great skill*

freefall—*to descend through the atmosphere for a time without the aid of a parachute*

immersion—*to be fully submerged underwater*

FIRST MANNED SOLAR-POWERED FLIGHT

The first manned flight using **solar** power occurred near Bakersfield, California, on May 18, 1980. The pilot was 13-year-old Marshall MacCready. The small plane weighed just 68 pounds (31 kg). MacCready's father founded the company that built the plane.

LONGEST LAWN MOWER RIDE

From 2000 to 2001 American Gary Hatter went on the trip of a lifetime by riding his lawn mower for 14,595 miles (23,488 km). He traveled through 48 U.S. states as well as parts of Mexico and Canada. Hatter's lawn mower traveled only about 9 miles (14.5 km) per hour. It took him more than eight months to complete the trip.

FIRST BICYCLE RIDE TO THE SOUTH POLE

Few people visit the South Pole—and even fewer get there by bicycle! In December 2013 Maria Leijerstam competed in the White Ice Cycle Expedition. Three people competed in this bicycle race across Antarctica to the South Pole. By winning the race, Leijerstam became the first person to ride a bike to the South Pole. Leijerstam's approach was unique. Rather than a traditional two-wheeled bike, she rode a three-wheeled **recumbent** bicycle. The trip covered 396 miles (637 km) in 10 days.

solar—*having to do with the sun*

recumbent—*a position in which a person leans back with his or her legs stretched out in front*

CHAPTER 3

ANIMAL ACCOMPLISHMENTS

People are great at setting new records. But animals often achieve wild feats too. Some animals set records for their natural abilities. Others set records for things they were trained to do. Take a look at some of the world's most incredible animal accomplishments.

LOUDEST PURR BY A CAT

Smokey was one loud cat! On March 25, 2011, this gray cat from Northampton, England, set the record for the world's loudest purr. At 67.7 **decibels** Smokey's purr was almost as loud as a vacuum cleaner!

decibel—*a unit for measuring the volume of sounds*

MOST TENNIS BALLS IN A DOG'S MOUTH

Many dogs love to play with tennis balls. Most dogs carry only one ball in their mouths at a time. But a dog from Dallas, Texas, named Augie carried many more. In 2003 the golden retriever gathered and held a total of five tennis balls in his mouth at once.

MOST MILK FROM A COW

Smurf the cow lives on La Ferme Gillette farm in Canada. In 2012 she broke the record for milk production. During her lifetime Smurf has produced more than 57,000 gallons (215,768 liters) of milk. That's about six times more than average cows produce during their lives.

LONGEST SKATEBOARDING DISTANCE BY A GOAT

One day in 2012 Melody Cooke's pet goat, Happie, jumped up on a skateboard. It wasn't long before Happie became a world record holder. She rode the skateboard for 118 feet (36 m). Many people were surprised, but Cooke wasn't. She said that Happie often does tricks like a dog.

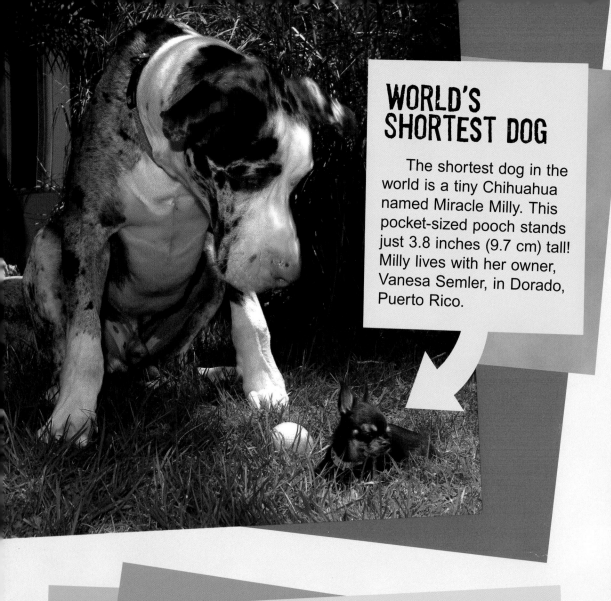

WORLD'S SHORTEST DOG

The shortest dog in the world is a tiny Chihuahua named Miracle Milly. This pocket-sized pooch stands just 3.8 inches (9.7 cm) tall! Milly lives with her owner, Vanesa Semler, in Dorado, Puerto Rico.

WORLD'S RICHEST PET

The world's wealthiest pet is a dog named Gunther IV. When German Countess Karlotta Lieberstein died in 1992, she left $372 million to her beloved German Shepherd, Gunther III. Then after he died, the fortune was passed on to one of his puppies, Gunther IV. The dog's fortune includes several homes such as the former Miami mansion of singer Madonna and a villa in the Bahamas.

MOST NUMBERS IDENTIFIED BY A HORSE

Karen Murdock has trained her horse, Lukas, to recognize numbers. Murdock places the numbers one through five on a board in front of the horse. Lukas then uses his nose to point to a number after she calls it out. In 2010 Lukas correctly identified 19 numbers in one minute as Murdock read them aloud.

LONGEST CAT FUR

Before he died in 2014, Colonel Meow had hair that reached 9 inches (23 cm) long. Owners Anne Marie Avey and Eric Rosario of Seattle, Washington, brushed him two to three times a week. Colonel Meow was a Himalayan-Persian mix. Persian cats are known for having especially long hair.

CHAPTER 4

MAN-MADE CREATIONS

What do an enormous whoopee cushion, a car made of cake, and an underwater hotel have in common? They're all record-breaking objects made by incredibly creative people. Let's discover some of the most incredible and bizarre things people have made around the world.

FIRST UPSIDE-DOWN STORE

Fashion designers Viktor Horsting and Rolf Snoeren don't just make unique clothes. They also built a one-of-a-kind store to highlight their clothing creations. From 2005 to 2008, they ran a store in Milan, Italy, that was decorated to look upside down. The ceiling was covered with wood flooring. Mirrors were placed high on the walls. And columns that should have started on the floor hung from the ceiling instead!

HAIRIEST CAR

In 2010 Italian hair artist Maria Lucia Mugno won the prize for the world's hairiest car. The Fiat 500 is covered with 220 pounds (100 kg) of hair. Mugno used all natural human hair to make her hairy creation.

WORLD'S TALLEST BUILDING

The Burj Khalifa building in Dubai, United Arab Emirates, is the tallest in the world. At 2,716 feet (828 m), it has more than 160 stories. It has an outdoor observation deck that's the highest in the world. The giant building includes apartments, office space, hotel rooms, a fitness club, and underground parking for 3,000 cars. It is more than twice as tall as the Empire State Building in New York City.

WORLD'S NARROWEST HOUSE

One home in Warsaw, Poland, is less than 3 feet (0.9 m) wide at its narrowest point. It was built in a narrow space between two tall buildings. The refrigerator can hold only two drinks. The dining room table seats only two people. And the bedroom can only be reached by a ladder!

WORLD'S TALLEST LEGO® TOWERS

In 2013 a group of students from Wilmington, Delaware, spent the entire summer building the world's tallest LEGO® tower. It measured 113 feet (34.4 m) high and contained more than 500,000 bricks! Not to be outdone, kids in Budapest, Hungary, helped build an even taller tower in 2014. The new record holder stands an amazing 114 feet (34.7 m) high. Both towers were built in small sections and put together with help from construction cranes.

WORLD'S LARGEST WHOOPEE CUSHION

Steve Mesure created the world's largest whoopee cushion. It has a **diameter** of 10 feet (3.1 m). It was made for the 2008 Street Vibe Festival of Sound held in London, England. The festival explored the role of science and engineering in making music and sound.

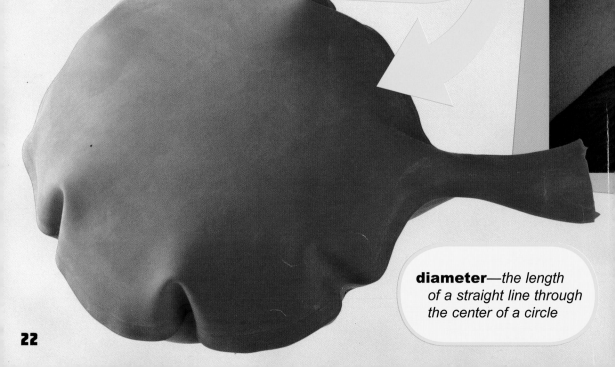

diameter—*the length of a straight line through the center of a circle*

FIRST UNDERWATER HOTEL

Built in the 1980s, Jules' Undersea Lodge in Key Largo, Florida, delivers exactly what its name promises. To reach the hotel, guests must dive 21 feet (6.4 m) under the sea. Despite the unusual entry point, the hotel has all the comforts of a normal hotel. It has hot showers, TVs, and even pizza delivery. However, guests must be certified scuba divers to stay there.

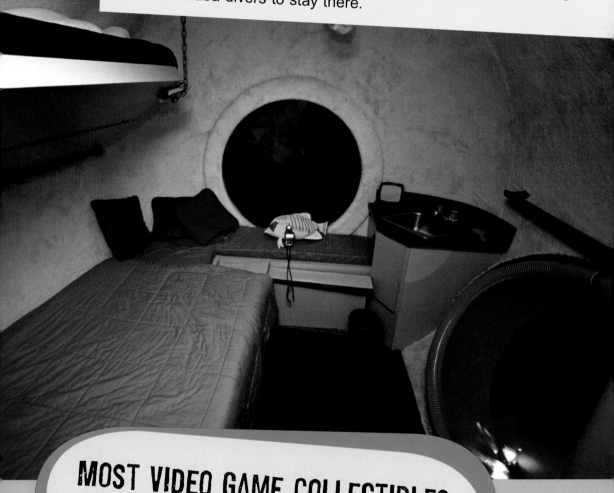

MOST VIDEO GAME COLLECTIBLES

Brett Martin has the largest collection of video game merchandise in the world. He owns 8,030 video game-related items. His collection is thought to be worth more than $100,000. The collection includes toys, figurines, controllers, stuffed animals, clothing, and many other objects. Martin even has a set of Mario-themed power tools!

WORLD'S LARGEST WALKING ROBOT

The largest walking robot in the world is a 51-foot- (15.5-m-) tall dragon. The radio-controlled robot has a 40-foot (12.2-m) wingspan and walks on four legs. It even breathes fire! German company Zollner Elektronik built the robot dragon for an annual festival in Furth im Wald, Germany. The festival includes a play about a dragon invading the town, which has been performed there for more than 400 years.

LONGEST MOTORCYCLE

In 2011 Colin Furze of Great Britain built the world's longest motorcycle. It's 72 feet (22 m) long and can carry up to 25 people. Its top speed is 35 miles (56 km) per hour. However, the motorcycle is so big and heavy that it's very difficult to steer.

FASTEST SOFA

Glenn Suter holds the record for the world's fastest sofa. The crazy motorized contraption has reached speeds up to 101 miles (163 km) per hour. The sofa even has a coffee table attached to it!

FASTEST EDIBLE CAR

In 2012 Carey Iennaccaro designed, built, and drove the world's fastest **edible** car. It was made of 95% cake. The frame, brakes, seat, and tires were real. But nearly everything else on the car could be eaten. Even the helmet Iennaccaro wore was made of chocolate and sugar. It could reach a top speed of 10.7 miles (17.2 km) per hour.

edible—*able to be eaten*

CHAPTER 5

WEIRD ACHIEVEMENTS

Some world records are awe-inspiring. Some are unbelievable. And others are just plain weird. One person set a record for burping! Another group of people set a record for brushing each other's teeth! Let's see what other really strange records people have achieved.

HEAVIEST WEIGHT LIFTED BY A TONGUE

In 2008 Thomas Blackthorne lifted an object weighing 27 pounds, 8.96 ounces (12.5 kg)—using only his tongue! Before getting the record, he had been lifting weights with his tongue for about 10 years.

MOST FEET AND ARMPITS SNIFFED

The Dr. Scholl's company is known for making foot care products. Madeline Albrecht used to do research for the company. During her 15 years there, Albrecht sniffed approximately 5,600 feet and countless armpits.

FASTEST TIME ENTERING A SUITCASE

In 2009 professional **contortionist** Leslie Tipton zipped herself into a suitcase in just 5.43 seconds. Tipton started bending and twisting her body at age 22. She admired the flexibility and training of acrobats who could bend their bodies in odd ways.

contortionist—
an entertainer who twists his or her body into strange positions

LONGEST BURP

Italian Michele Forgione was responsible for the world's longest burp in 2009. The epic belch lasted an amazing 1 minute and 13 seconds!

MOST PIERCINGS

With 453 body piercings, Rolf Buchholz of Germany has more piercings than anybody else in the world. He has more than 100 piercings on his face alone! Rolf is also a big fan of tattoos. His whole body is covered in tattoo art.

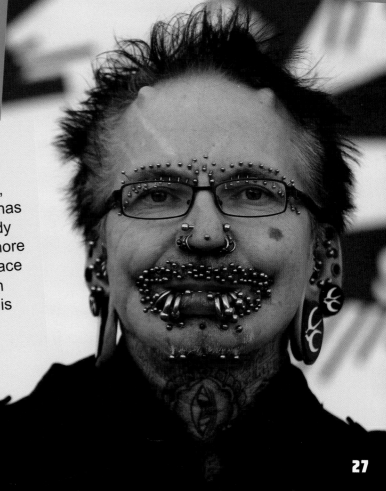

LARGEST GAME OF MUSICAL CHAIRS

The world's largest game of musical chairs took place in 1989 at the Anglo-Chinese School in Singapore. The game started with 8,238 participants and took three and a half hours to finish. The winner was 15-year-old Xu Chong Wei.

LARGEST TOOTHBRUSH CIRCLE

In a toothbrush circle, several people stand in a circle and brush the teeth of the people next to them. Camp Kaylie in Wurtsboro, New York, holds the record for the largest toothbrush circle. In 2013, 126 people brushed one another's teeth at the same time.

LARGEST UNDERWATER WEDDING

The world's largest underwater wedding took place at Jaworzno, Poland, on August 27, 2011. The marriage ceremony was attended by 303 divers and lasted about 18 minutes. The happy couple and the priest communicated using plastic-coated paper and sign language.

MOST PEOPLE HUGGING TREES

In 2013, 951 people gathered at Hoyt **Arboretum** in Portland, Oregon, to hug trees. They had to all hug trees at the same time for a full minute. To beat the previous record, organizers asked random visitors to join in the effort. One woman who got married that day even hugged a tree in her wedding dress.

arboretum—*a place where scientists and other people study different types of trees*

LARGEST TUG-OF-WAR TOURNAMENT

In September 2012, 1,574 students competed in the world's largest tug-of-war **tournament**. The event took place at the Rochester Institute of Technology in Rochester, New York. It was part of the school's annual Mud Tug tournament. More than 150 teams participated. The event raised more than $10,000 for charities.

tournament—*a series of matches between several players or teams, ending in one winner*

GOING FOR THE RECORD

Humans are driven to achieve great things. For some people it means running the fastest mile or creating a beautiful piece of art. For others greatness comes by knitting underwater or balancing ping-pong balls on their chins. Thousands of people try to break crazy records every year so the rest of us can marvel at their incredible achievements.

GLOSSARY

acrobat (AK-ruh-bat)—a person who performs gymnastics acts that require great skill

arboretum (ahr-buh-REE-tuhm)—a place where scientists and other people study different types of trees

contortionist (kuhn-TOR-shun-ist)—an entertainer who twists his or her body into strange positions

decibel (DE-suh-buhl)—a unit for measuring the volume of sounds

diameter (dye-AM-uh-tur)—the length of a straight line through the center of a circle

edible (ED-uh-buhl)—able to be eaten

freefall (FREE-fawl)—to descend through the atmosphere for a time without the aid of a parachute

genetic (juh-NET-ik)—relating to physical traits or conditions passed down from parents to children

immersion (ih-MUR-zhuhn)—to be fully submerged underwater

lisp (LISP)—a speech problem that causes a person to incorrectly pronounce certain letters, especially "S" and "Z"

pituitary gland (pih-TOO-i-tayr-ee GLAND)—an organ that influences many body functions, including bone growth

recumbent (ri-KUHM-buhnt)—a position in which a person leans back with his or her legs stretched out in front

solar (SOH-lur)—having to do with the sun

tournament (TUR-nuh-muhnt)—a series of matches between several players or teams, ending in one winner

READ MORE

Morse, Jennifer Corr. *Scholastic Book of World Records 2014.* New York: Scholastic, 2013.

Ripley Entertainment, Inc. *Ripley's Believe It or Not! Special Edition 2014.* New York: Scholastic, 2013.

Time for Kids editors. *Top 5 of Everything: Tallest, Tastiest, Fastest.* New York: Time for Kids, 2013.

INTERNET SITES

FactHound offers a safe, fun way to find Internet sites related to this book. All of the sites on FactHound have been researched by our staff.

Here's all you do:

Visit *www.facthound.com*

Type in this code: 9781491420157

 Check out projects, games and lots more at
www.capstonekids.com

INDEX